PRAISE F
CAPTIVATING BENEFITS

"Well put together, clear, concise, great anecdotes—100 percent sells the idea of the alternative, and basically points out how an organization would be crazy not to consider this path. Very, very persuasive."

—Joe Hollingsworth
Vice President, Ascot Group

"The book is very thought compelling about where we are and where we are going. I'm hoping we can go in the direction you suggest. Every year we battle huge increases for less coverage!!"

—Bob M
COO of a Bucks County Hospitality Business

"I've been struggling with this issue for twenty years and it's like everything this book described is how I've felt all this time. When can we start."

—Terry B
Founder/Owner, Multi-Site
Delaware Valley Retail Organization

CAPTIVATING BENEFITS

CAPTIVATING BENEFITS

CONVERTING VICIOUS TO VIRTUOUS*

Rejecting the vicious cycle of ever-increasing commercial health insurance premiums in favor of a safe and time-tested, self-funding alternative.

Joseph Reardon HCAA - CSFS

For the brave people in this industry who recognized when the ACA was passed that something new had to be created. Their wisdom and perseverance have presented us with a gift of opportunity.

CONTENTS

FOREWORD

by Anthony D. Cellucci Jr., CEBS
The Beacon Group of Companies

Over the past thirty-plus years the cost of health insurance has steadily increased but the level of actual insurance coverage has steadily decreased. Imagine paying more for a brand-new car that doesn't drive as well and costs more to maintain than that same exact car purchased two years earlier. Unfortunately, this is what's happening to the health insurance purchased by small and midsized companies for their employees. Until recently, we had no real solutions other than instituting plan design and premium contribution adjustments or moving from one carrier to another every few years. Sometimes these solutions serve companies very well, but far too often they leave the midsized companies with little to no potential of realizing the rewards they'd otherwise experience in a partially self-funded arrangement.

Thankfully, there is now a solution about which qualified employers need to be aware: an employee benefits captive within a partially self-funded arrangement. For many midsized employers across the country, this approach presents an excellent opportunity to proactively stabilize the cost of providing health coverage to employees. Member companies realize scaled-up buying power and program enhancements otherwise unavailable on a stand-alone basis.

In the pages that follow, Joe explains how America's

healthcare insurance marketplace arrived at this point and what employers can do to prudently and proactively end the unjustifiable premium increases once and for all. Joe entered the group insurance business thirty years ago working for insurance companies, group Medicare programs, pharmacy benefits managers (PBM), and benefit consulting firms. Joe has a passion for helping employers and employees take control of their health insurance spending and improving their overall experience with their insurance when medical care is needed. The targeted end result is increased employee appreciation, retention, and improved hiring outcomes.

As disrupters advocating for employers and employees, we ask questions such as:

- Why aren't employers sharing in the savings generated by lower claims costs in those years when claims run well?
- Why is it not explained that receiving a premium surplus rebate is a clear indication the employer is being overcharged?
- Why can't midsized companies across the country join together to obtain the preferred pricing larger companies enjoy?

Joe answers these questions in an easy-to-understand manner and provides the steps to follow that may lead to employers and employees becoming much healthier, both physically and financially.

PREFACE

For about the last ten years, I have been a small business owner in a way that is completely unrelated to my professional career. I'm fortunate those ventures are profitable and require little of my involvement. I do not put myself in the category of a person running a business with hundreds of employees, but having invested a significant amount into starting something from the ground floor, I do have experience with skin in the game and where the difference between success and failure has real consequences.

I was tipped off to a book called *The Seven Basic Plots: Why We Tell Stories* by Christopher Booker who worked on it for over thirty-five years. The two giants in the field of human behavior are Freud and Jung. Booker was a Jung disciple, and his book is regarded as a significant piece of work, and I was blown away by it. The shorthand version is that people react and respond to storytelling like it is coded into us as a feature of our behavior. The notion of a story, poem, movie, etc. "moving us" refers to this subconscious form of programming where we can become changed. More amazingly is that every story ever told is a derivation of only seven plots: overcoming the monster, rags to riches, the quest, voyage and return, comedy, tragedy, and rebirth. The commonality is that all plots include a hero who is navigating through the plot line(s) and advancing with the assistance of a guide. I think of Daniel and Mr. Miyagi, Luke and Obi-Wan, or perhaps Rocky and Trainer Mick.

I reflect on the amazing amount of overlap of this idea to my own path. I was midcareer with young children and the thought of starting and/or owning a business while holding down my career wasn't something I seriously considered or knew how to do. It is stunning when I think about the number of times it was true that the "teacher appeared" when the "student was ready."

I bring this up because you're running a business with skin in the game and you sometimes lay awake at night with the weight of knowing the livelihoods and well-being of a lot of people hinge on decisions you make . . . you are already a real-life hero. I mean that sincerely. An executive who carves out the bandwidth and allows themselves to be guided on understanding how to fix their employee health plan once and for all is pursuing an endeavor of such consequence that I struggle to find examples that compare in relative importance.

Selling more of what drives revenue is a great strategy and a worthy goal to have every year. But isn't it true that sometimes an adjacent "fix" will end up being the biggest win you will have? You will always—I repeat, *always*—need a tool for attracting and retaining the employees *you want*. Having a high-performing health plan is a gift that will keep on giving.

This book is offered as a story intended to move you. You've been on a certain path for some time now and have awakened to the realization that maybe you are not happy where you are. And inflation and competition for talent are rubbing salt in the wound.

These chapters will guide you in a new direction, one where employers hear their once-resentful employees say things like "We can't tell what you're doing different, but it's working . . . and I wouldn't want to work anywhere else."

INTRODUCTION

I'm a contrarian by nature and I've lived long enough and seen enough to know that no person, process, or organization is perfect, but I do believe the midsized employer community constitutes the best of America, and I feel obligated to do everything in my power to improve the well-being of as many such organizations as I can. There is a great thing happening regarding self-insurance for midsized employer health plans, and it is accessible to far more people than are presently aware. I'm speaking specifically about the concept of a group-benefits-captive insurance program for midsized employers, which replaces what I will now refer to as carrier-centric group health insurance or the traditional programs marketed by the Blue Cross Blue Shield, UnitedHealthcare, Cigna, Aetna—BUCA for short—and distributed through a network of commission-based benefit brokers. Out with the old, in with the new.

The underpublicized reality is there is a community of thousands of employers across the country who are now succeeding wildly after having reached rock bottom. The very early adopters had the fortitude and courage to try something over ten years ago before it could be proven to them that it would work. The results of ten-plus years now make clear that it is a superior offering and a game-changer for employers and employees alike.

With my degree in mathematics and a concentration in actuarial science and statistics, I was good in math but not good enough to achieve standing in the Society of Actuaries. I entered the insurance industry in the '90s working for an HMO, which led to a role with a consulting firm and a stretch of twenty years dealing with large employers and their strategies for providing benefits to employees. I've had positions in client management, sales, and consulting for companies like Aetna, Express Scripts, and Mercer. In short, I had my natural analytic capabilities and a lot of acquired knowledge and experiences regarding how the biggest and best employers went about things.

Beginning with a role I accepted in 2015, it represented my first exposure to what I will call the middle market and I was baptized by fire; it seemed like all I knew from twenty years or so was suddenly not applicable because of some key differences between large and midsized employers.

The good news is that what I subsequently learned—and it keeps being refreshed—is what makes up the rest of this book you're about to read. I should say that I relearned these things because they have always been true and always will be. I relearned that *necessity is the mother of invention*, that *the only thing to fear is fear itself*, and that *where there is a will, there is a way*. And I learned that the midsized employer community is light-years ahead regarding creativity, determination, and grit. I'm thrilled to be able to supply my career experiences to bridge the divide for midsized employers so they can experience the same rewards as larger companies.

In the US, there are over nine hundred thousand licensed health insurance agents, and I'm one of only about seven hundred who are certified self-funding specialists (CSFS) via the Health Care Administrators of

America (HCAA). It takes credibility to succeed in this field, but it also takes common sense. I believe if something is broken, stop doing it. Luckily, I found a strategy that works and can show you how. It has been the biggest thrill of my career to repeatedly hear self-insured midsized employers say, "Thanks for pushing us. Now we can see there wasn't anything to fear . . . I wish we would have tried this sooner."

Chapter One

The Most Important Thing Is the Most Important Thing

Okay, so what is it? The most important thing is your employees (and their families and/or dependents) and the relationship between them and your organization. If that's not true, you wouldn't be reading this far. The business you run needs them and the good work they do, and you offer pay and a package of benefits that add security to their lives, which accrues goodwill to you the employer. That's the goal, but does it ring true, or does it ring hollow? Do they value their benefits, or are they confused by them? Do you understand the power that benefits have to help, confuse, or worse, even hurt your employees?

The first thing that must be acknowledged is the system of employer-provided benefits contains structural problems that we have to understand before we can address them. But if you are a long-frustrated employer, I must point out that the current system is not capable of saving you. Where our minds need to go is in the direction of new solutions that have incentives that align with us and include safeguards to make sure incentives will always align with us. It would not make sense for us to agree that a system is broken and then go about implementing a replacement system that does nothing but mimic or build upon the prior method. Imagine your mechanic saying, "Here's your car back, it runs the same as when you brought it in."

First and foremost, the words involved have gotten muddled. A good deal of the American public conflates the idea of health and health-care insurance. Let me ask this: if you could only have one thing, would you rather have your health or a health insurance policy? Perversely, today's typical health insurance policy becomes more meaningful and necessary, as more people do not cultivate and nurture their own personal health and well-being.

The ideal would be where the health insurance policy behaved more like other forms of insurance such as homeowners and auto insurance, where the policy owner covers the routine upkeep (of their house, their car, their person), and the policy is there for things that would be catastrophic or generally too much to pay out of pocket. But I'm getting ahead of myself a bit.

How did we get to where we are now, where there is general frustration and disillusionment around health-care benefits and the cost of health-care services?

During WWII, the United States government instituted wage controls hoping it would stabilize the workforce since a large segment of workers were now overseas in battle. The rules exempted employer-paid benefits, meaning this was how employers on the home front ended up competing for talent. To attract employees, employers started offering more and better (i.e., richer) health benefits. This is the beginning of the problem, the uncoupling of the relationship between a service and the cost of providing the service. There is no area in life that we spend our own money where we are as clueless about cost as we are regarding health care–related services.

We're sheltered from prices and focus on certain types of care, and providers make money by treating the sick. This means that if a population were healthy and strived to preserve their health in all possible ways, the health-care industrial complex would experience anemic economic activity. Opaque pricing has large consequences since almost none of us (including doctors and hospitals) know how much we pay for care or how much the care costs to provide.

This anecdote is from a 2018 *Wall Street Journal* article, entitled "What Does Knee Surgery Cost? Few Know, and That's a Problem," and illustrates the underlying problem: For nearly a decade, a Wisconsin hospital boosted the price of knee-replacement surgery—the most common non-childbirth procedure in the US—an average of 3 percent a year until the list price (billed amount) was more than $50,000, including the surgeon and anesthesiologist. Yet even as administrators raised the price, they had no real idea what it cost to perform the surgery. They admitted using a combination of educated guesswork and a *canny assessment of market opportunity* (emphasis added). To their credit, and somewhat due to their embarrassment around this situation, the organization pursued an eighteen-month study to determine their actual all-in cost to perform the knee surgery, and it was about $8,000, not $50,000.

The absurdity of this story is unfortunately true and

scary once you get your mind around the implication. It can and should be extrapolated into every service performed by every provider in every facility in America. While maybe not all the results will be as outrageous as this one, many are worse.

The current US employer-provided health benefits system is based on overuse, overtreatment, overcharging, and overpaying, and it will only stop when those who are being negatively impacted decide they won't put up with it anymore.

Like the proverbial frog in the slowly boiling pot, millions of small decisions have contributed to the dysfunction and resulted in increases in utilization, which has led to increases in costs, all the while we have undervalued what keeps us healthy and allocated very little in the way of resources to it.

In case you had any hope that technology would bail us out, health care seems like the only industry where technology has produced higher costs and lower productivity. Usually, it arrives and drives down prices and improves efficiency. No such luck.

It is possible to view the last fifty years as a slow-motion hyperinflation crisis in the making. Like most crises, as German macroeconomist Dr. Rubi Dornbusch stated, it "takes longer to form than you think it would, then happens much faster than you thought it could." What makes it an actual crisis is that as the system's failure becomes apparent to more and more people, enough will start figuring their way out before (they hope) it's too late. With fewer remaining "in the payer pool," they end up paying even more to make up for the shrinkage of the base, and the problem spirals out of control.

Illustrating the scope and size of today's health-care

inflation problem, consumer-goods prices have increased eight times in the last fifty years while health-care prices have increased 274 times and the hyperinflation has taken from nearly every group and segment of society—blue collar, white collar, executives, frontline staff, rich, poor . . . it doesn't matter.

In terms of recent history, the way midsized employers procure their benefits programs is by way of an intermediary advisor, such as a benefits broker. The midsized company is in the business of making and/or selling certain products or services, and they rely upon subject matter experts like CPAs, investment advisors, and insurance brokers to supplement the successful operation of the enterprise.

In the case of health insurance programs, there are regional variations that must be understood to know why a broker in Pennsylvania or New Jersey might act differently in supporting a client than a broker in Texas, Louisiana, or Wisconsin (just to pick a few states away from our immediate region) would.

Certain areas of the United States can be identified as carrier centric versus others that are employer centric. Why is this, you ask? Well, for the same reasons there is any kind of regional variation or why some states are red and some are blue, or why some are right-to-work and some are more unionized.

In the mid-Atlantic and Northeast, we have long been carrier centric. Regarding health insurance, the mid-Atlantic and Northeast lay of the land has been the insurance carriers (i.e., BUCA) are the center of the universe selling their fully insured programs through their broker network. The process is straightforward. There is no complicated "underwriting" involved per se, and the employer simply pays a fixed rate based on their eligible employee census multiplied against their actual monthly enrollment per employee tiers, and each annual renewal is a ratcheting upward in terms of a premium increase, and no one ever gets a premium decrease.

The carrier typically has a pharmacy benefit management (PBM) subsidiary "carved in" to their offering, and it becomes another profit center for them. The carrier does everything from contracting with and managing the PPO network, processing medical and Rx claims, performing disease management and member services, etc. If what I just described sounds to you like convenience, I understand that point of view. But what tradeoffs or shortcomings result from gaining that convenience? We'll discuss those later, but now let's talk about employer centric.

In many regions of the country, TPAs rule, and carriers are almost nonexistent in the midsized employer market. A TPA is short for a third-party administrator, and the core of the TPA's role is to adjudicate doctor and hospital claims as well as handle member-service inquiries. Equally important is that the TPA, in conjunction with the benefits broker, plays a quarterback role in designing, building, and maintaining the employer health plan. TPAs typically offer an array of options to employers for them to select which they favor most. Employers can plug and play different PPO networks, different PBMs, different disease-management vendors, etc. The TPA's value proposition is the opposite of "one size fits all." They create a platform that enables clients to determine what works for them, and the TPA is nimble in adapting to when things work or when things don't.

The big difference is that TPAs engage with employers

who "self-insure," and TPAs are not considered to be insurance companies. They do not file with the State Department of Insurance because they are not selling insurance products. TPAs offer what is known as "stop-loss programs," where stop-loss is a form of insurance but focuses on catastrophic claims and, when packaged correctly, establishes the plan sponsor's maximum liability and is no less safe than a fully insured program. Self-insured employers fund their claims as they go along instead of paying a fixed premium amount to the carrier. Periodically, the TPA reaches into the employer's funding account to access enough dollars to cover the provider claims for the prior time frame, and all is reconciled.

So what do people who self-insure their health benefit programs using TPAs and stop-loss insurance know that those of us in a carrier-centric area such as the mid-Atlantic and Northeast don't? Are they "right" to do it their way, and we're "wrong"?

I could go a few directions with this but a big reason for the discrepancy is that a mentality has been entrenched over a long period of time, a process has been accepted, and there have grown to be a huge number of people who feed off the status quo in our mid-Atlantic and Northeast region. Pennsylvania, with focus on the greater Philadelphia marketplace, is unique in how carrier centric it has been over generations. Not long ago, there were four fully insured Blue Cross Blue Shield plans in Pennsylvania (though there are now three); Aetna has a sizeable fully insured presence in large part to the legacy of US Healthcare; Cigna was headquartered in Philadelphia for many years; and UnitedHealthcare has been aggressively pushing into this market for at least the last dozen or more years.

So what gives? It's dollars and cents. From my days

working inside the big carrier, the rule of thumb from a revenue perspective was somewhere between eight and ten to one for fully insured versus self-funding. In other words, the carriers bring in eight to ten times more revenue for being sellers of health insurance plans compared to simply being an administrator of a self-insured healthcare program.

In very large part, fully insured is promoted not because it's in the employer's interest but because it is in the carrier's interest. The carriers have sophisticated units which capture time-value of money on the large premium amounts that they collect upfront. Claims take time to process and even include the carrier collecting additional money from employees after the copays or coinsurance has been calculated during claim adjudication. After a lag in time, the carrier issues provider payouts, which is the first occasion money has left their door. Prior to paying the doctor or facility, the carrier earned spread income, which is called "maximizing the float." Because the book-of-business premium numbers are so big, the investment spreads don't need to be large or for long before it adds up to real money.

Brokers are paid commissions by the carriers, and as premiums increase, so does the broker's commission. It doesn't get more complicated than that to see why they might not be the ones volunteering to "ring the alarm bell." The short story is that this region has been proliferated for a long time with large insurance carriers who, in conjunction with their established process and their network of intermediaries, have gone along and gotten along while the employers paying the bills were expected to just keep paying more and more. Paying more every year without a rationale is bad enough, but you the employer have been put into an unwinnable position where you are without tools other than to shift the cost increases onto your employees by way of raising their copays and deductibles. The symbiotic broker-carrier relationship has no concept of what your annual squeeze feels like and the pressure you are under to simply hold it all together. They just want to shake hands with you on the renewal, bury it all, and hope you forget how miserable the process is by the time next year rolls around.

I hope it now makes sense why the whole thing feels as awful as it does. It's because it has been created by numerous parties to benefit themselves and, if anything, stifled innovation and hoped you wouldn't notice or complain. Offering benefits probably has felt a little like a necessary evil, something you knew you didn't like but had to go through with anyway.

I'm not here to naively tell you I can make problems disappear. Health care, the cost of health care, how your employees feel about their benefits are all topics we will be discussing for the foreseeable future. What I have access to is a solution that has been built by employers like you, for employers like you. It has been created to include flexibility and customizability and to ensure that every feature aligns with your vision as an employer and plan sponsor.

In this book's foreword, Tony mentioned that finally a new alternative had arrived in the form of an employee benefits group captive ... and that is what I'm talking about when I say, "built by employers like you, for employers like you." One of the key things necessary for an employer to take advantage of this opportunity is their mindset. I have found that when we get access to decision makers in midsized businesses who have had an arms-length relationship with the company's health-care program for one reason or another, and we present them with a conceptual overview of the employee benefits group captive, the most common reaction is, "That makes so much sense! Why doesn't everyone do that?" Up until recently, the financial and operational executives have not been advised about the emergence of this solution, leaving it all to be figured out by the HR representatives.

The following are words from 2012 and come from the CEO of one of the first companies to join, what is today, the nation's largest employee benefits group captives and which happens to be headquartered in Philadelphia. The program they joined as an early adopter in 2012 has added more than two thousand employer groups and is fast-approaching a million covered lives in the subsequent ten years. The CEO had finally had one too many pound-the-fist-on-the-table moments and commandeered the decision-making from the HR team. When considering to stay the course and keep playing the game or try something else, the CEO concluded, on the podcast *80/20 with ParetoHealth*, it was time to be bold: "I trusted my consultant, who brought the new solution to my atten-tion . . . but I was skeptical at first. In the end, the terms weren't perfect but were good enough. I didn't need to know what my worst-case scenario was going to be because the best-case scenario was way better than anything I had and the worst-case scenario was the same as what I was used to."

CHAPTER TWO

BUILD OR BUY?

Because the focus of this book is on midsized employers, let's spend some time describing the features of a midsized organization. Businesses that have made it to "midsized" status have survived a variety of growth stages, and it is important to understand this history when we analyze successful strategies of big businesses compared with solutions that some midsized employers haven't had the confidence to consider . . . but should.

STAGE 1

In the beginning of any business, the "existence" stage is the point in time when the owner/founder did everything, and the focus was on getting customers and making enough money to pay bills. These early days don't involve much in the way of systems or formal planning; it was a daily effort to do what needed to be done and hope there was some money left over. You could almost simplify it into "the owner was the business."

STAGE 2

It's a fight for survival and follows a period when

enough time has passed that the company didn't fail. Many that will ultimately fail do so quickly. The key problem shifts to "How well can we manage revenues against expenses to achieve profitability?" The business structure is still very simple, and while there may be a sales manager or a general manager at this point, they would not be able to make critical decisions without the express agreement of the owner. There remains little that is systematized yet, and survival is still the thing that occupies the most headspace.

STAGE 3

The "success" stage is where the owner/founder is faced with questions about their ambition and what they want for their business and its future. The business has achieved profitability, and now is the time when the owner must decide whether to pursue growth and expansion or remain stable/profitable.

By this time, the company has functional managers to take over duties from the owner. The managers are still subservient to the owner because of the corporate structure, and by extension, the manager's upward mobility is limited. The company strives to learn how to stockpile money while things are good so it might withstand an inevitable rough time, whenever that might come.

STAGE 4

This is the stage where those companies that chose to grow pulled it off—they have grown, and this is the first time where the business gets into delegation. Can the owner delegate successfully in what is now an increasingly complex enterprise?

By now the key managers must be very competent to

handle a growing and complex business environment. Systems are now refined and extensive, and *operational* and *strategic* planning processes involve specific managers and are no longer "fly by the seat of your pants." The owner and the business have become effectively separate entities, no longer indistinguishable from each other, but the company is still dominated by the owner's presence in multiple ways.

If the business is successful in moving from Stage 4 to Stage 5, this is where an entity has the potential to become an enduring big business.

STAGE 5

"Resource maturity" refers to the fact the company has the staff and financial resources to engage in detailed operational and strategic planning over a multiyear time horizon. The organizational structure has turned departmental, and management is decentralized as well as being adequately staffed and very experienced. Systems have advanced to be very extensive and well developed. The owner and the business are financially and operationally separate. There is no rule for how long a period all of this has taken, but this is the point where the company has "arrived" and has the advantages of size, financial resources, and managerial talent.

BIG BUSINESS VERSUS MIDSIZED EMPLOYER

This book is about a strategic process for midsized employers who want to address the third largest expense in their organization and do so in a way that improves the employee benefits program and makes them an employer of choice, able to attract and retain the employees they want.

I'm not going to try to diagnose what stage your company is in, but what if we approach it by comparing your organization to one with resource maturity? What are the most meaningful differences?

BIG BUSINESS

Very large employers self-fund their employee benefits health-care program almost all the time.

Companies that Self-Fund Health Coverage

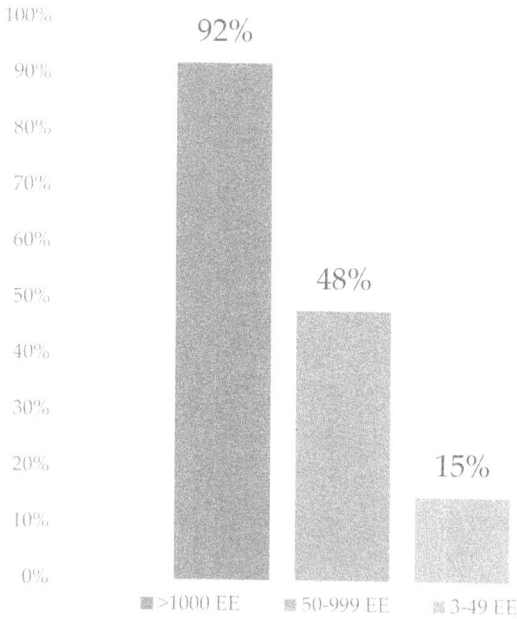

▓ >1000 EE	▓ 50-999 EE	▓ 3-49 EE

Source: Kaiser Family Foundation

The most common scenario for the >1,000-worker firm is they have a multi-person HR team, potentially including an analyst, manager, director, and VP, and they work to assess the market with guidance of a large national or dominant regional HR consulting firm. The company's HR department has a budget, and their success in contributing to the overall organization is measured by comparing their realized results versus their departmental goals outlined by the CEO and the board during the budgeting process. The critical factor is that because the HR department is tasked with meeting a budget number, they strive only to implement programs and solutions which contain strategic flexibility and can be dialed up or dialed down as necessary. So, in other words, the tool the large employer prioritizes over all others and retains at all costs is *control* and they achieve control by being willing to self-fund or self-insure the benefit programs.

MIDSIZED EMPLOYER

Regarding the companies that we deal with, and who are the focus of this book, the approach usually is not "departmental" but rather involves a combination of roles/people serving in a way as an ad hoc benefits committee:

- HR manager
- CFO/controller
- owner/founder/president

When talking about the ways companies attract and retain employees, we should always begin with the health-care plan the company sponsors because that's what employees tell us.

Top Benefits When Considering a Job Decision

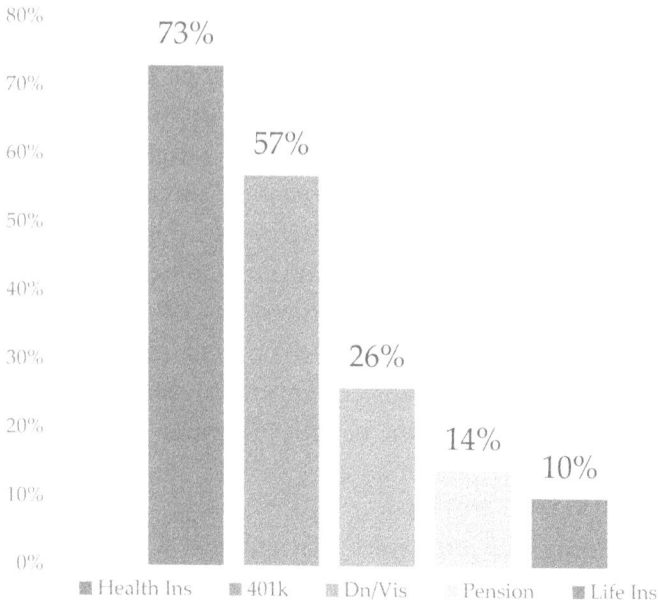

80%	
	73%
70%	
60%	57%
50%	
40%	
30%	26%
20%	14%
	10%
10%	
0%	

▨ Health Ins   ▨ 401k   ▨ Dn/Vis   Pension   ▨ Life Ins

Source: Employee Benefits Research Institute and Greenwald & Associates

There is an old saying about a committee that set out with a goal to draw a horse and ended up drawing a camel because, well, they were a committee. Unfortunately, the "hybrid committee" approach used by many midsized employers to develop their benefit programs results in being unfocussed, confused, non-confident, and passive rather than "detailed," "strategic," "extensive," or "well-developed," which are buzzwords used to describe the resource-mature organization.

Because most midsized employers do not have a permanent department to focus on this area all year, the hybrid committee only comes together for a few weeks, in a rush to make certain decisions, and tends to be deferential about transferring the understanding of "what's going on" to the broker or the intermediary advisor/expert. The intermediary expert in the midsized employer scenario is often a local broker instead of a national firm and sometimes has their own business considerations regarding short-term versus long-term strategic thinking. I do not place blame on anyone for this arrangement but see it as an example of human nature at work. The stretched-thin staff thinks, *I've already got too much on my plate. The broker is supposed to be the expert; I'm fine with whatever they say.* And the local broker is often perfectly okay following the regular process and handing it over to the insurance carrier and collecting their commission—no fuss, no muss. In this example, nothing improves; the cycle continues and people grow more and more frustrated.

Within midsized employer organizations, the key executive in the ad hoc committee is often apprehensive and lacks the confidence to engage much at all. They may even approach the subject with concern about the impact on themselves or their family as health plan participants. Some executives maintain a low profile to avoid awkward family dinner-table conversations if, heaven forbid, any plan changes made at work to try to improve the performance of the overall plan were to somehow result in administrative headaches for the executive's significant other and/or children at the time and place they were attempting to access health benefit–related services. They made a trade-off that staying with the undesirable status quo was preferable to getting critiqued at home if they were deemed to have contributed to a snafu, even if it was well intended. These executives feel as if they have people whose job it is to handle this stuff, and besides how bad could it really be? An organization that fits this profile commoditizes the health plan and figures one carrier is just as good as any other and will move around every few years, getting them all to compete against each other on price. The HR staff is, on one hand, happy the executive stays out of it but is also dispirited about the process because it is unfulfilling. HR is the place where employees bring their frustrations about the rising cost of payroll contributions, the increase in deductibles and copays, etc., and they don't have any good answers to give. Employees are tired of hearing it just as much as HR is tired of saying, "We have the Blue Cross Blue Shield/United/Cigna/Aetna/Anthem PPO program, and it's supposed to be one of the best around; there is nothing more we can do."

What I am trying to call attention to is *the nature of the mistake*, which results in the health plan never getting fixed once and for all. The midsized employer, who finds themselves stuck in the annual merry-go-round with the BUCA carriers, has made the mistake of giving up control to their broker advisor and to the insurance carrier and very specifically *by NOT self-insuring* the health plan. There are advisors to work with and programs to implement that are as safe or *safer* than the carrier-centric packages, but they require the employer to recognize that they must break their own pattern of behavior that has been grooved over many years.

The midsized employer is *not* wrong to believe that they should join a risk-sharing pool to make up for not having the law of large numbers on their side. After all, a company with one hundred employees enrolled in its plan would not be smart to assume the risk as if it had two thousand employees enrolled. The midsized employer's error comes from forfeiting the control to an insurance carrier who feels they should be paid a premium in exchange for security since they are holding the risk. The employer who gives up this control loses the ability to manage a number like their large-employer counterparts.

WHAT THE MIDSIZED
EMPLOYER SHOULD DO IS BOTH:

a) join a risk-sharing program (i.e., an employer benefits captive); and
b) self-insure.

This chapter's title is "Build or Buy?" which is a turn of phrase every business owner probably understands. The process of starting up a small business, assisting it to grow, and then helping it improve involves countless occasions for figuring out solutions to problems. The problems don't all look or act the same, and neither should the solutions. We used to joke that my dad was a one-tool handyman. Whatever problem there was around the house, it was going to get hit with a hammer.

A business handyman is hopefully more skilled and nuanced but inevitably exists in the mode of thinking to themselves, *To fix this problem, do I have to build something or buy something?* That's where "build or buy" comes from. In reality, "build" could be as simple as understanding that we need to roll up our sleeves and figure the problem out, and "buy" could mean hiring someone on a short-term consulting assignment who has a certain skill set we need right now but we don't need forever, or it could be more literal, such as *Should we build a new warehouse or buy one that already exists?*

In the context of solving employer-provided health

benefits, I think it helps to frame the discussion in this "build or buy" context.

We can only consider this problem to be solved if our employer clients deliver an offering their employees love and that reflects goodwill back to the business. Anything short of that means we have yet to fully fix the problem. We want our clients to hear employees tell them, "We love what you're doing, and we wouldn't want to work anywhere else."

And we want our clients to approach their employees in a new way—dare I say, a dialogue. The conversation could start out like this (this is a bit wordy but could come in an "announcement of change" communication):

> *We realize the annual benefits enrollment process has not created what we wanted, and you've told us the same. We have decided to change course, and we have a favor to ask. We promise to be forthcoming about what we're doing and why, and we ask for a little bit of patience.*
>
> *Our goal is to stop taking more each year out of your paycheck to cover health plan enrollment and to stop shifting toward higher deductibles and copays. To do this, we're changing the way things have been done for a long time. Operationally speaking, if we do our part exceedingly well, you might not notice many changes at all, besides the part about keeping more of your money. All we are doing is "self-insuring" our plan instead of relying on an insurance carrier even though you will retain access to the carrier's network of providers (doctors and hospitals).*

*We're doing this because we've been intro-
duced to a process that thousands of employers
like us have tried, and we've spoken to these
organizations . . . and the results have been
consistently amazing. What excites us most is
that employees report loving the new process as
much as the employers. Employers who have
been practicing the new process over a few years
tell us they keep getting better at it, and employees' appreciation also grows over time because
of the results. We're heading in this direction
because we see the opportunity for a significant
"win-win," so we're going for it.*

This is the "build" mindset. Not every problem or
challenge calls for a "build" solution, but I would say with
the ones that are closest to the heart, the ones you can't
afford to get wrong, the very best solutions will more often
come from the "build" than the "buy" because you're
more invested in making sure it's done right.

CHAPTER THREE

FOMU OR FOMO

Let us begin with a story that was captured in the October 2014 edition of *The Self-Insurer* by Bruce Shutan, a seasoned reporter who has written for several human resource trade publications, including *Employee Benefit Plan Review*, *Human Resource Executive*, *Incentive*, *Plan Sponsor*, *Risk & Insurance*, *The Self-Insurer*, and *Workspan*.

The article begins by depicting a telephone conversation between a midsized-employer client, and a property-and-casualty (P&C) insurance captive manager. The two had a successful collaboration over the years, where the captive was able to control cost and deliver a better solution compared to traditional products in the workers' compensation marketplace. This particular phone call was the client venting about spending $100,000 on workers' compensation insurance but as much as $1 million on benefits and wondering, *Why does the benefits market seem to have no strategy to get health care to look like workers' compensation?*

The two parties on the call had an epiphany: What if the promising P&C group captives that worked so well at the time for workers' compensation could be replicated for the employee benefits space? And so, it began. This marked the beginning of a real alternative to the status-quo carrier-centric, nonfunctioning marketplace that midsized employers have been forced to work with for generations.

In 2012, the parties on that phone call began down a road, which by 2023, looks quite different. These employers stared down their fears and decided to move forward into somewhat of an unknown. Their "Fear of Messing Up" (FOMU) was a lesser concern than their "Fear of Missing Out" (FOMO). Regarding the phone-call scenario depicted in *The Self-Insurer* by Bruce Shutan, this has grown into the nation's largest employee benefits captive with well over two thousand such groups banded together, representing a "covered lives" headcount the size of Seattle, Charlotte, or San Francisco. All these name-recognizable cities have populations of roughly eight hundred thousand, and so does America's largest employer health-care group captive. Since the starting days of 2012, according to ParetoHealth, over 97 percent of the groups that put their FOMO ahead of FOMU and signed up to participate have remained in the program. Hardly anyone has regretted the decision. And those that want to exit are permitted to do so with no strings attached. There are no golden handcuffs utilized to keep the program together.

Participating employers when asked about how they "broke out" of the old way of doing business and got into the new arrangement, routinely say the same thing, some variation of the following:

> *We were skeptical at first, but we did our homework and decided to try it. It couldn't be*

worse than the other way if we were careful. After being in for a while, we now understand how to make it work for us better than we did at first. We love it and so do our employees. We only wish we started earlier.

These bold folks were the classic early adopters, or the people who decided to "build" their solution instead of buying. They had the instinct to tap into something at a gut level that I think is important to understand. These executives were able to see through the fog and arrive at a moment of realization. They realized they were victims of a false premise. The premise that existed was that midsized employers needed to play it safe when it came to offering a health benefits program to their employees. But these employers woke up to being very much not safe. They started to think of their health-care plan—which is the company's second or third largest expense—as if it were a piece of their day-to-day business. What is the right way to deal with a supplier where the costs go up faster than the ability to overcome them and where there is no transparency or accountability from the service provider? The questions almost start to answer themselves. Anything would be better than that.

So let's talk for a second about the Fear of Messing Up (FOMU), this powerful force that has kept too many midsized businesses stuck in a failing process for too long.

Let's shift away from employer-provided health-care benefits and consider FOMU in other realms of our life. Because I'm talking to seasoned businesspeople, I now want to take your mind to areas other than your business. Where does FOMU creep in and influence what you do or don't do?

Let's pick a few examples to see how we handle not letting fear keep us stuck. In these examples, I'm using family members, but the idea is relatable to a business owner or executive and the paternalistic relationship to their employees. Your oldest child is nearing college age, and they've asked you to help identify where they should go to school. Right off the bat, it should be obvious that your response would not be to say, "I'm afraid I might mess it up for you. I'll have to sit this one out." No, you are honored to have been asked to play this important role, and you care deeply about getting it right because it will have long-lasting implications for you and your loved one. It's time to roll up your sleeves.

It's easy to start out being overwhelmed with all the considerations of "seeing your baby grow up" and the prospect of them going off on their own, possibly far from home, on top of the financial ramifications of college tuition. Heck, it's been so long since you went to college you wonder if any of the process is the same or if your knowledge of how to do this is up to the task.

Because you are a good and thoughtful parent, you will proceed calmly and soberly through a series of information-gathering steps. Timing will be key—you won't want to wait until midway through your child's senior year of high school. You will have thought out how and when they take the ACT or SAT and if they should pursue prep classes and study groups. You might even hire someone who has precise experience helping kids find the right university and knows how to navigate the process. You'll fill out applications for a reasonable number of schools (since each application costs money), and preferably, you'll have a sense ahead of time where their chances of acceptance are good.

All of this is to say, you will put in the homework and follow a process and adjust along the way until you decide. The work done along the way serves to eliminate a Fear of Messing Up. Knowing you weighed out the pros and cons of the various possibilities leads to confidence.

Don't be the person who did none of the above and waited until it was too late after the colleges had issued all their acceptances and then had only the scraps from which to choose. I can easily see that person thinking, *Boy, I really messed this up*, and rightfully so.

Or maybe it has come time to consider the living arrangement of an aging parent. Once again, we choose an example involving a close relationship and where getting the correct answer is important. This scenario is similar in that it also includes doing research and not waiting. In this case, the parent can't walk up and down stairs very well anymore, and there is no lavatory on the first floor of the home, which, even though it is a shrine, can no longer be maintained. We're under a time crunch to resolve the situation to avoid a bad fall everyone knows is inevitable if we're not quick. Here, again, we gather as much information as possible and talk to people who have experience: *What can we afford? Will the parent be accepted? What kind of living assistance is available? Can we visit any time we want?*

In either scenario, or any similar example, the queasiness in your stomach doesn't go away entirely once you've decided. You might wish you could perfect the process and remove any possibility of things not working out. Being around the block a few times has taught us that is not how it works. As Teddy Roosevelt, the twenty-sixth president of the United States, once said, "Do what you can, with what you've got, where you are."

Shift back now to making a business decision that will have great benefit to your company and your employees. At this point, I could go to the previous paragraphs and just cut and paste. It's about timing and putting in some homework and talking to those who are on the path already. You can decide to change or not. But Fear of Messing Up should be eliminated as a reason for inaction.

As you think about other employers with whom you compete for talent, whether in your region/town/community or industry, it might be worth considering how formidable they would be if they were ahead of you in the process of fixing their health-care problems. If your chief business rival had a high-performing health plan their employees absolutely loved, how complicated would that make your life? Not only is their business not overspending, making them potentially more profitable than you, but their employees are not overspending, making them hard to hire away or hard to hire in the first place.

This is where I like to instill the Fear of Missing Out because it *should be* a motivator. It's good to fear missing out on something others are doing if it could be good for you also. As it's been said, fortune favors the bold. Companies don't get ahead of their competition by accident. They find out about opportunities, and they take advantage of them. They see openings, and they exploit them.

CHAPTER FOUR

UNDER THE RADAR IS SUDDENLY TOO BIG TO IGNORE

From the vantage point of anyone trying to run a business, cost predictability is incredibly important and especially so for midsized employers. By definition, a midsized firm is not resource mature and hence can't buffer a "missed number" quite like a big business can. For any business, it makes sense to head into a new year with the goal to sell more than what was sold the year before. But if the other part of the equation, the costs to produce what you sell, isn't well understood or under control, it's conceivable that in some situations it would be better to "sell less" because you'd be losing money on each transaction. It would be better to stop the bleeding first.

I say all that to illustrate how important cost control is and to segue into how it relates to the current situation and employer-provided health benefits. It can't be denied that the strategic play of managed care (HMOs and PPOs) effectively solved a problem for many employers in the 1980s and 1990s.

The HMO/PPO model achieved cost certainty and financial efficiencies mainly by eliminating unnecessary hospitalizations and forcing participating physicians and other health-care providers to offer their services at discounted rates, in exchange for which the carrier would steer the members to the in-network providers. The primary care provider (PCP) played the key role and was compensated to quarterback the delivery of services and was incentivized to retain as much of the member's care in their office versus outsourcing to a specialty provider or hospital. The logic was that PCPs were equipped in a low-intensity office setting to handle a very high percentage of health needs and referrals to more complex settings, which would drive up the cost and were done as a last resort.

By 1993, according to J. Iglehart's article, "Physicians and the Growth of Managed Care," 51 percent of Americans receiving health insurance through their employers were enrolled in managed health-care plans where a PCP gatekeeper was involved with the process of issuing referrals for more complex care. Eventually, stories involving benefit denials of medically necessary services began to be commonplace and led to a public outcry, so the tide was turning against these once-popular programs. Many states passed laws to try to enforce managed-care standards and limit abuses associated with denying services.

The rest of the 1990s was a legislative effort to curb managed-care organizations; somewhere around nine hundred state laws governing managed-health practices were enacted. A system that was based on a sound premise was starting to be chipped away at because, in practice, there were legitimate operational flaws that led to serious concerns. A careful observation of the fatal flaw was that managed-care companies pushed the PCPs to do more and see more patients while offering their services at progressively deeper discounted rates. The PCP doctor was the person upon whom the system depended, and they were being worked harder and harder just to keep pace, and the managed-care firms were heavy handed in terms of the amount of scrutiny in overseeing physician's behaviors and were interpreted as infringing on their clinical judgment.

By the end of the 1990s, the public had soured on the mechanics of managed care (referrals, denials, etc.), and the providers who made it work were experiencing severe burnout. When the 2002 movie *John Q* arrived, Denzel Washington was a big box-office draw, so the movie left a mark. It was poorly rated by those who reviewed it, but it was noted by Roger Ebert for "pounding the audience over the head with its [anti-HMO] message." The timing was right, where the mood of the people and notoriety of the film seemed to solidify the public's consciousness that managed care was a worthy villain and the HMO/PPO industry was permanently changed.

That's not to say insurance carriers disappeared—they did not—but they did change their tactics. In the 1990s, when managed care was flourishing, it was indisputable that to achieve the lowest provider rates was to have the smallest network. The providers who were willing to participate knew that in exchange for slashing their regular prices, being "the only dermatologist in the network" meant a virtual guarantee they would do well based on membership steerage. From the perspective of a doctor's office being a business at the end of the day, they benefited from not needing to market their services or build their practice organically if they signed a deal and relied on the managed-care organization for patient volume.

The flip side of this is that the public had come full circle and learned to hate the idea of the "small network," so what were the insurance carriers to do?

For the last fifteen or twenty years, the insurance carriers still have "networks of providers" and still claim that having providers contracted in their network is the way they achieve the best discounts to pass along to their clients and their members. What it amounts to is a bit of a game being played.

The insurance carriers know that the public believes "the bigger, the better" in terms of the network. The public doesn't want referrals or to find that any of their providers are out of network. And the insurance carriers know that most employers, especially midsized employers, don't want the blowback of a workforce who thinks they're being shoehorned into an HMO plan or a similarly restrictive managed-care plan from yesteryear.

What is the result of this? The insurance carriers all went about building as big a network as they could and had no leverage. Especially in the Delaware Valley region, the dirty little secret is that every provider is more or less in every insurance carrier's network. The providers all know the insurance carriers are no longer building small networks, so why offer up deep discounts? Providers who had been reluctant before now could simply ask for the rates they wanted and often got them. After all, it's not the insurance company's money. To them, it's your money. This happy marriage between the provider community and the insurance carriers has resulted in a *contract* no longer being the thing that provides assurance for the controlling of costs. Studies have been done which validate that commercial PPO contracts are driving up costs rather than containing them.

In a previous section, I referred to midsized business executives, who, truth be told, would love nothing to do with their company's health plan but felt they had to get involved. Their intuition told them something fishy was going on. This is what I was talking about. I deal with this topic every day, and I try to help as many people see the light as possible, but I'll admit, I get some funny looks when I explain to someone that a PPO contract between a doctor and insurance company is increasing cost, not controlling it.

I have also stated in this book that the current system has been built in such a way that it can't save you if you are someone in the camp of "currently waiting for things to get better." Things can't get better because the foundation of the traditional carrier-centric model is fatally flawed.

The insurance carriers will continue building large networks because employers and employees alike don't want restrictions. Providers know this and will continue to look for higher prices. Anyone who doesn't understand that this is how the game is being played will continue being burned and somehow confused about what's happening.

The following table shows Pennsylvania's top three insurance-carrier-membership totals since 2011, and in gray is the sum of all carriers' membership. The chart depicts that the fully insured large group (101-plus employees) market is figuring it out, and it is shrinking. People like me, and the message we carry, are breaking through. This is true in many states but especially so in

Pennsylvania, where the Kaiser Family Foundation has found that enrollment has steadily shrunk by a total of 35 percent in nine years. These results don't mean the members disappeared; it means they've moved from fully insured to self-insured. They had the light bulb go on, and they acted.

As fully insured pools continue this pattern of shrinkage, it will place more burden on the bitter-end groups that are not getting out for whatever reason(s).

Fully Insured in **Pennsylvania**

	TOTAL	Highmark	IBC	CBC
2011	2,405,329	766,542	633,937	234,918
2012	2,259,436	803,883	560,504	221,444
2013	2,169,077	788,764	504,187	267,908
2014	2,003,997	685,359	491,988	265,392
2015	1,825,043	655,480	430,319	235,848
2016	1,763,813	618,365	396,137	199,521
2017	1,671,033	583,165	344,438	219,385
2018	1,557,863	617,615	303,462	161,077
2019	1,552,396	609,455	308,106	173,219

Kaiser Family Foundation: PA Large Group Fully Insured Market (101+ employees)

This is what I call a problem that is suddenly too big to ignore if you remain on the merry-go-round and hope your insurance carrier partner will figure it out sometime soon.

The process of a midsized employer being able to safely self-insure their medical program and to shift away from the carrier-centric version came about for real in the 2012 time frame, as described in Chapter 3 of this book. That just so happens to line up nicely with the table. This fully insured carrier-centric market is contracting, and the self-insured captive model is growing in roughly equal numbers over the same period.

CHAPTER FIVE

RESULTS MATTER

Let's put the final nail in the coffin for those who think the broker-BUCA strategy might finally come to its senses and save the day.

The story I'm about to tell regarding Walmart, the largest private employer in America, was detailed in the *Wall Street Journal* article "To Curb Wasteful Health Spending, Walmart to Send Employees Traveling for Spine Surgery."

Walmart, with its unlimited resources of time, people, and money, undertook a process of evaluating the healthcare spending of its workforce. For one thing, they wanted to save a bunch of money, but they also were looking to gain insights or market intelligence for the purpose of developing products to be commercialized for revenue. There is rarely only one reason why a Walmart store gets involved in a project like this in such a way as we're about to describe.

While getting very granular with their employees' data, Walmart noticed a certain percentage of their employees were utilizing "low-skilled" providers within their carrier-partner's network. Physician skill, like many other skills or professions, can be measured on a bell curve, where there are noticeable outliers on either extreme and generally 80 percent tend to cluster in the middle. Said another way, 10 percent are high-skill, 10 percent are low-skill, and 80 percent gravitate around the mean.

In the case of health-care dollars and where skill is important, it often involves facility settings and procedures such as complex surgeries, which require the patient to be admitted for an in-patient stay of some duration before being discharged. In this case, a high-skilled physician/provider is one with a high percentage of successful interventions as gauged by low incidents of complications and/or readmissions.

In Walmart's case, they approached their carrier with a proposition that they believed the carrier could make operational and which would automate that Walmart employees would receive care from only skilled or high-skilled providers. It was a simple request—or so they thought. They asked, "Please create a custom network for our employees that eliminated the low-skilled providers from consideration." To do this meant whenever steerage was to take place, a Walmart employee would be able to avoid ending up with an inefficient, less-skilled, and probably more costly provider. The carrier said, "No." They denied the request and cited their "all or nothing" contracting philosophy. The contract either includes all providers or none. For any group or employer that seeks to drive down costs, one must be able to identify where care can be received most efficiently and then steer employees in that direction whenever possible. If they couldn't count on their insurance carrier's help, you probably shouldn't hold your breath either.

But wait, didn't we just learn their request was denied and they were stymied? So, what did they do? Yes, the partner with whom they had a history of "buying" their health-care solutions turned them down. So, they shifted into "building" mode to find their solution. They got into the details of self-administering, for a short period of time, a program that paid for surgeries at big-name systems while reducing the payments for local providers. The theory was that incentivizing as many employees as possible to a Mayo Clinic (for example) would have a reliably better financial result. For employees who chose to seek care, closer to home, their cost-share was higher. They did not mandate anything but provided options for which there were clear financial motivators to serve as the steerage.

Similar to the Walmart case is a well-detailed case study on the Allegheny County School Health Insurance Consortium in the Pittsburgh area as detailed in *The CEO's Guide to Restoring the American Dream* by Dave Chase. It demonstrates the power of steerage within self-insurance and what "builders" can do when they put their mind to it. A consortium of schools wouldn't automatically jump out as an ideal candidate for such a creative approach, but such was the nature of their situation. It was exacerbated by a local and prolonged battle between the dominant carrier and dominant provider system in the Pittsburgh market.

The group, like everyone else in the region, was caught in the middle, and it was turning out to be ugly, and the public negotiations went on for a while. The school consortium had no choice but to try to do as much as they could to help themselves while the two behemoths were consumed with battling each other for all the public to see. They started to look at data, much like the Walmart analytics team did, and saw huge utilization figures at the number one–ranked, highest-quality facility in the region and quite a bit at the twenty-third–ranked facility as well. They crafted a program intended to shift utilization, and the following charts show the results. The lowlier-ranked facility had a quite high utilization before the steerage program was implemented but saw their activity reduced by two-thirds, and the group in total swung their financial results by almost $12 million in a single year.

Before

| #1 Hospital in Region, (highest quality rating) | • over 33,000 services performed
• nearly 300 admissions
• just shy of $5,000,000 in total costs |
| #23 Hospital in Region, (low quality rating) | • over 31,000 services performed
• over 360 admissions
• just over $15,000,000 in total costs |

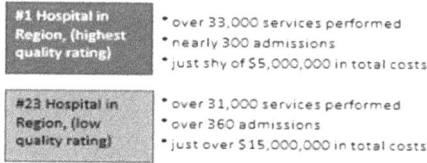

The Intervention

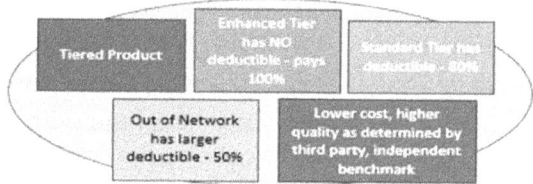

Tiered Product — Enhanced Tier has NO deductible - pays 100% — Standard Tier has deductible - 80% — Out of Network has larger deductible - 50% — Lower cost, higher quality as determined by third party, independent benchmark

After

| #1 Hospital in Region, (highest quality rating) | • over 40,000 services performed ⬆ 20%
• 328 admissions ⬆ 9%
• just over of $7,000,000 in total costs ⬆ 40% |
| #23 Hospital in Region, (low quality rating) | • over 6,600 services performed ⬇ 70%
• 113 admissions ⬇ 70%
• just over $5.5 million in total costs ⬇ 60% |

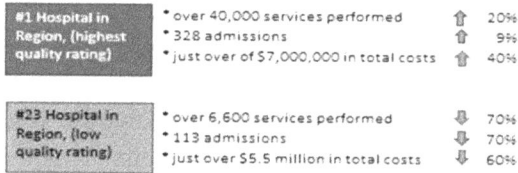

The entity had budgeted for a $4.5 million deficit but instead turned a $7 million profit (a swing of almost $12 million).

If you want to know how the subject of employee benefits can become something magical, here is what the employer offered to employees for the next year due to their amazing results (found in *The CEO's Guide to Restoring the American Dream* by Dave Chase):

- Payroll deduction for health-care premiums plus 1.9 percent (very low by current standards)
- Enhanced Tier has NO deductible (100 percent paid)
- PCP visit with $0 copay
- Specialty with $10 copay
- EAP provider is included in the cost
- Second-opinion provider is included in the cost

This is what makes it possible for a new kind of relationship between employer and employee. The employer has "built" something of value and when it works as intended, and as planned, they can offer back to employees, which creates a virtuous (not vicious) cycle and a two-way flow of goodwill.

These are tangible results that came from the employers and their advisors taking matters into their own hands and not playing along with the carrier-centric mentality. The good news, and what makes this possible, is that the size of the population of employers, like the two mentioned above, is not small.

As of the turn of 2023, thousands of employers have changed their mindset and probably changed their advisor(s). It's true that some advisors are not bullish on self-funding for their midsized clients, and many know little to nothing about group captives. It requires skills and a new way of doing business, to which they may not want to adapt, especially the further along they are in their careers and after becoming comfortable with the usual ways for so long.

This is where I reiterate a point I have made a few times along the way. The longstanding system with a symbiotic relationship between the broker and the insurance carrier is set in its ways and neither of those parties can be counted upon to reinvent themselves. Short of an employer making their own mind-set shift, the existing system can't and won't save anyone in it.

The largest of the insurance carriers did not take seriously the threat that their fully insured customer base would leave them. It is no doubt they leaned on the adage of "relationships matter," and every midsized employer has a broker that was their fraternity brother, neighbor, wife's brother-in-law, etc. I think this attitude reflects more than a little arrogance, but I will also admit it is mostly accurate. In the end, those who denied the possibility that a competitive model could emerge greatly underestimated the will and the spirit of the people who populate this segment. There were and are simply too many people who:

a) know when things "don't add up";
b) know how to get things done;
c) don't take "no" for an answer;
d) don't give up until the job is done;
e) don't like being taken for granted;
f) and finally had enough.

The following chart excludes Aetna because CVS Health purchased them in 2018, but it does show the other national carriers' public stock prices over the ten years following the passage of the Affordable Care Act. You read that right—they were trading in the area of $50 a share in 2010 and all the way up to $500 a share by 2023.

Stock Prices
Aetna was excluded due to being purchased by CVS Health in 2018.

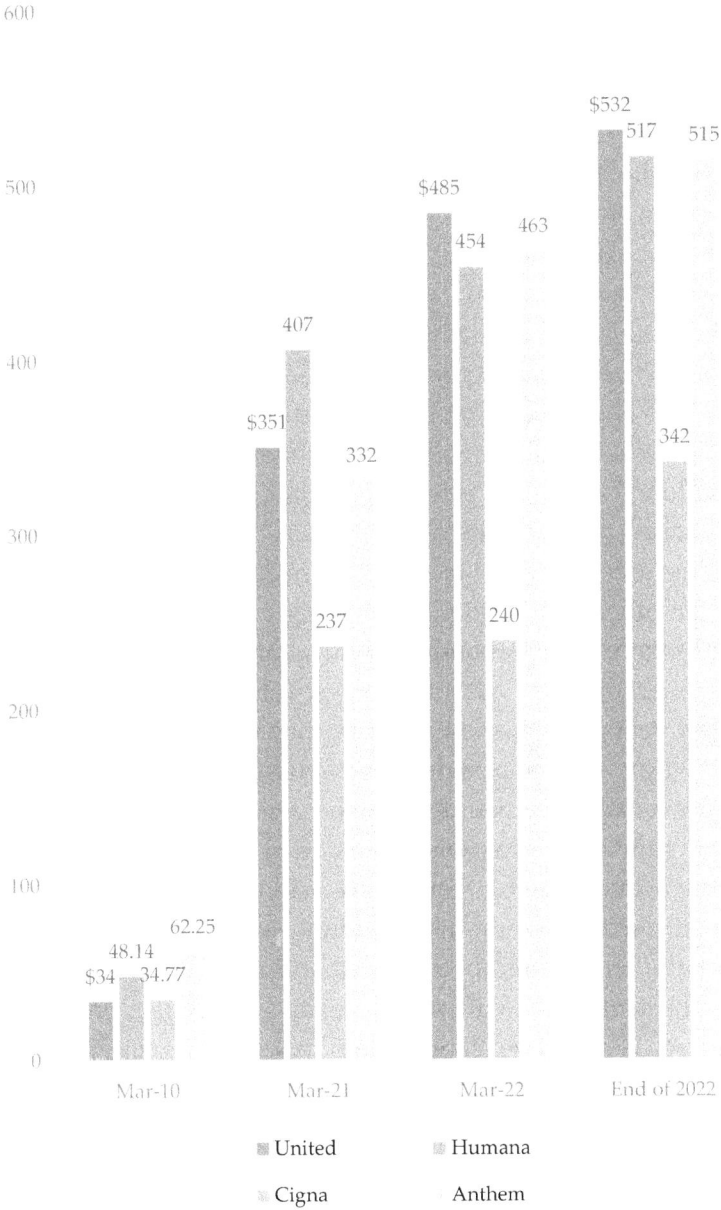

	Mar-10	Mar-21	Mar-22	End of 2022
United	$34	$351	$485	$532
Humana	48.14	407	454	517
Cigna	34.77	237	240	515
Anthem	62.25	332	463	342

■ United ■ Humana
■ Cigna Anthem

It's no wonder the executives at these companies did not feel like they needed to cater to midsized employers or drastically alter their way of doing business over the last decade. Numbers like those in the chart tell executives to "stay the course . . . keep doing what we're doing." As a midsized employer, have the last ten-plus years been that kind to your business?

In the boardrooms of UHC, Humana, Cigna, and Anthem, I do not think there was a lot of lost sleep on whether ABC company, with its 150 employees (covered on the health plan), would have to forego issuing Christmas bonuses because the renewal for the coming year is higher than expected and hadn't been budgeted.

That is precisely the level to which I like to draw the conversation. Get away from them. Come join the "builders" who are now a population the size of San Francisco or Charlotte and will help buffer your plan's claims and give you the scale you need. Let us guide you in the process of building something you can be proud of and everyone in the company will want credit for creating. I've seen this play out a few times. When the company is a few years into the new process, they forget how bad the old way was because it doesn't matter anymore, and there is universal agreement that the new way is far better. All of a sudden, it was everyone's idea to do it. Nobody remembers dragging their feet or asking if it was going to mean extra work or the seemingly endless number of "what if" questions about fears that didn't materialize.

The truth is it will take a leader to get the process started. Will you be "that leader" for your company? You might have been reluctant before, but you continue to feel in your gut that there has to be a better way, and you are right.

Chapter Six

Long-Term Solution

According to Duke University's CFO survey, over 80 percent of midsized employer executives say health-care spending is one of their largest expenses. Close to five out of six executives say this is true. Being a top expense means that a problem with benefits is a problem for the business. Such a high number also suggests it's going to be a key issue facing businesses for a long time coming and requires a solution built for the long haul.

As the gatekeepers of a company's resources, it is ideal for senior executives to take a proactive role in crafting the health benefits strategy of their organizations, including reviewing health-care plans as part of their annual strategic-planning process. Four out of five finance executives surveyed said having a best-in-class health benefits plan was essential to meeting business objectives, further reinforcing that benefits and business are inseparable. With rising costs and tightening budgets, managing an employee health benefits plan is more than ever falling under the purview of CFOs, presidents, and owners/founders and less reliant on human resources.

While this shift is real and has been happening for some time now, there is still plenty of room for progress for many employers.

Bob G. is the CFO of a commercial bakery with 550 employees using a self-insured captive plan. Bob believes the CFO's role in evaluating health benefits cannot be underestimated. As he explained in the Duke survey, HR is usually concerned about offering the actual packages to employees and educating them on coverage and benefits. But when it comes to cash flow and the total cost of a self-insured plan, all oversight falls to the finance division. "The financial planning of health benefit plans is a very important part of my job as CFO, and it's up to me [to] forecast and mitigate any financial risks to the company," he said.

Part of the CFO's role is to understand the cost-benefit of any investment or budget item. Too often, "planning" next year's benefits consists of a single annual renewal meeting where a broker presents a spreadsheet comparing an assortment of undesirable options. With renewal deadlines looming, employers are forced to make hasty and partially informed decisions. In the absence of long-term strategic planning, the process simply repeats year after year in a series of helpless, powerless renewal transactions.

When surveyed, many executives (over 65 percent) agreed that it would be beneficial to their business if they could find a way out of these types of reactionary decisions. An overwhelming majority (85 percent) of executives reported that it would help them understand the cost-benefit analysis if they had access to real-time data around pharmacy costs and health claims.

Health Plan Key Strategic Considerations

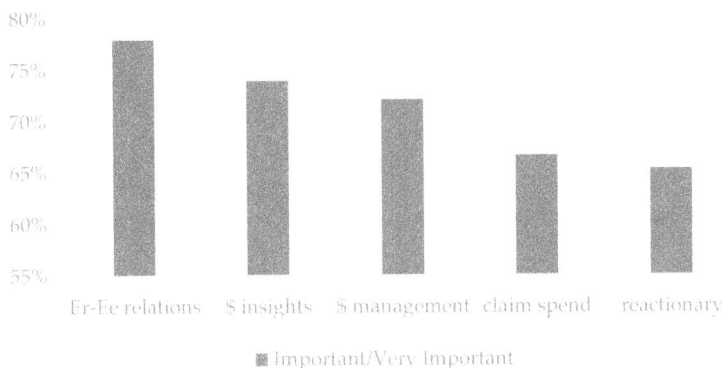

The group captive solution gives the executive the ability to exit the hasty renewal process by having continuous access to monthly real-time data so there no longer are mysteries about "how the plan is running."

This chapter concludes with a series of encouraging anecdotes from those who are living in the new solution daily after having their "mad as hell and not going to take it anymore" moment. A few times I have stated the group-benefit-captive solution is loved by employers and employees alike. This is completely true but what has impressed me the most might be the group benefit captive's ability to reinvigorate a sense of purpose for a variety of roles within the employer's organization. Nobody likes going to work to push paper or do busy work with no tangible sense of making a difference. The project of installing a high-performing group-benefit-captive health-care program, with a trusted advisor as your guide, will unlock avenues of growth for employees as they begin to grasp the importance of their contribution and how it directly improves their situation as employees as well as the company's financial well-being at the same time.

Talk about a contrast to the old way of procuring benefits with the carrier-centric model and their inflexible manner where it was the definition of pushing paper. If they're being honest, everyone involved in the old process was feeling like they were just going through the motions.

The purpose of this book is to move you into action. As I've gotten to know prospects over the years, one of the best things I have to offer is the ability to facilitate their attendance at an in-person event made up of hundreds of existing group-benefit-captive members. Participating member companies meet annually; think of it like a shareholder meeting. Since prospects are people too, they have ranged from wanting me to chaperone and make all the introductions to others wanting to explore on their own so they could be unsupervised and find out if there is any hocus pocus going on.

I can say the following without reservation: I've been in the business of employer-provided benefits since the mid-1990s and I've attended myriad conferences and seminars, too many to count. When I walked into my first group-benefit-captive member meeting, I was blown away. I had never seen so much positivity and enthusiasm, and I'm talking about an event including thousands of people over multiple days. Sure, it was a warm-weather location and people were letting their hair down (all the usual stuff), but what I'm talking about is the guts of the event, the presentations and the breakout sessions, and the working groups. The focus and intensity were real and different from anything I'd seen. There was no "going through the motions" happening in this place.

I remember writing at the time that I had seen "health-care reform" in action. Not a mandated top-down version of reform but a grassroots, common-sense, durable version. I place this program in a rare category. Even as a cynic by nature, I can't find much about it that I don't approve of and like. I scrutinized it from every angle, looking for the holes in it myself, and I came up empty. My feelings are so overwhelmingly positive that I decided to grab on tight. I want to help employers grab on too, and I plan to devote the rest of my career to helping as many as I can.

You will notice the following cross-section of endorsements contains a variety of roles and titles from real people whose companies adopted captive self-funding.

Marilyn B, CFO and benefits coordinator for a one hundred-year-old, veteran-owned manufacturing company— "Having great benefits make the attraction part easy, but retaining our existing employees is actually more important." The primary goal of the plan is to keep employee costs low, she explained. "With a forty-dollar monthly cost, they don't have to focus on health issues or stressful insurance bills. I need my employees to be 100% focused when they're at work, so the more I can do from a health benefits perspective to reduce stress, the happier and more productive our employees are."

Don H, VP of HR at a real estate and parking investment business—"It's a new day being part of a captive. Getting the real information every month with our claims data, getting inside strategies on what we can to head off our claims and modify our plan to respond to employees' behaviors and their use of the plan, how we can get people to use it to improve their own health, and providing truly win-win solutions."

Bill S., SVP of operations—"The benefits employees see are the tangible ones of keeping the costs flat. When we can improve the plan benefits, that is clearly something they appreciate. Employees that have been at another company and experienced what the annual process is and are used to the 8–10 percent increases and so when they come here and experience something different it does make a big difference. We actively use it to recruit"

Phil S., COO of a one hundred-year-old, eight-state law firm—"We really believe the group captive model is the future of benefits. We are excited and vocal about it because we believe so much in the program and the participants and the third-party partners that we're associated with. We just want to tell people, 'Get away from the fully insured model. It's nuts. It doesn't make sense. While maybe it's easy, it's a lazy approach to your number two expense on your ledger.'"

Tony R., CFO of a forty-year-old construction ESOP—"We were fully insured like a lot of people . . . the same story. Very dissatisfied. Once a year, the broker would show up with some Christmas treats and give you the bill and tell you how hard they fought for you, and it just felt like something was missing. I didn't have the experience before but I just kept asking questions knowing there had to be a better way. What are we doing wrong; what are we doing right? We had no data. We just didn't know. Eventually, we found the idea of the group benefit captive."

Bob F., risk manager at a Global Asset Management firm—"The group benefit captive eliminates the upper-level risk because they're watching your back with good cost-containment products. You've also got the support to keep those huge spikes that you get when you have a bad year, the captive eliminates those."

Julie G., director of HR at a seventy-five-year-old multistate, family owned bakery—"We strive to be an employer of choice . . . we try to be a company of integrity and respect." After years under a fully insured plan, the company had grown restless and dissatisfied. They were missing the insights they needed to impact their quality of care and get more value from their spending. "We wanted to better understand how we were spending our money and how our money was being spent. We were looking for options to navigate the world of health insurance and find better ways to spend the company's money that would actually help our employees. The resources that the captive has given us—the thought-provoking ideas, the knowledge-base building—have really complemented everything we wanted to do. It has been a tremendous partnership for us. It has been a blessing to be able to be part of the program . . . We saved more than $6 million over the first three years. Our actual claims are a lot less than we budgeted. We thought we'd see savings a couple of years out, but we've seen the return on investment every year since we joined."

CONCLUSION

In my introduction, I mentioned that the aim was to avoid being a technical how-to manual but rather intended to persuade you into action.

Chapter Two went a little bit into the stages of growth following the formation of any business. When summarized the way that I did, it doesn't give a sense of the amount of time involved. For sure, it doesn't happen overnight that a startup advances to a resource mature big business. One thing is for sure though—each subsequent step along the progression is less certain to occur and is more complicated than the previous step. The early-stage development can be accidental and serendipitous in both good and bad directions, but intentions become increasingly more critical over time as the business evolves.

There is an old saying in business that getting to the next level sometimes requires different partnerships and went something like "The people who can help shape your new tomorrow are not the same people you're working with today." Whether we're talking about an accountant, a business advisor, a financial advisor, or even a mentor, it is conceivable for a growing and evolving business to require new perspectives. This isn't a statement intended to be critical of anyone, it's just the nature of things.

That has been the central theme of what I've written. First and foremost, the topic of the health-care benefit program being offered to your employees is bigger than a regular but nagging administrative issue even if the critical factors are somewhat intangible. Try to resist falling into the trap that many are in. As a key decision maker, you will be tempted to stay in your lane, but this issue spans the entire business and affects most of the employees, so it warrants your attention. Second, there has been a model in place for a long time that is hopelessly broken and incapable of self-correcting. If it is true that the advice you have gotten along the way has not highlighted the predicament in the way I have in this book, I humbly submit it is time for you to seek new perspectives.

Your organization may or may not have big ambitions, and there is nothing wrong with companies that prioritize profitability and stability over growth and expansion. Regardless, no business should miss chances to be more efficient and in sync with employees when opportunities arise. Not grasping the importance of the major shift this book has outlined relative to employer health care will increase the likelihood your business will incur more pain and dysfunction and a further deterioration of the employer-employee relationship.

It's not uncommon for health-plan participation to cost a family something nearly equivalent to buying a new car every year, and that's just when we count the payroll deductions and the high deductibles. In other words, before the plan of benefits even kick in, before you the employer has paid anything at all, the employee has shelled out an enormous sum of money. You can start to see how some employees view the health plan as a burden rather than a benefit. Employers who keep kicking this can down the road risk a growing backlash. How well can a business with resentful employees compete with companies where there is genuine goodwill and transparency? I don't think they can for long. Genuine goodwill and transparency have the added benefit of being realistic and achievable and will stand the test of time.

There is no magic involved in this process, and it doesn't make challenges disappear. What we do is take a certain amount of energy that has been directed at this problem in the past, and we reconfigure how we use it. The negative energy that didn't solve anything in the past can now be deployed creatively in the future and gives us a shot at something very good and is a real win-win for the employer and employees alike. We create a new playing field with a legitimate shot at realizing very good results versus staying put and having almost no shot at winning or even seeing improvements.